To.. Aunt
Kenlyn
From.. Kim

Christmas '04

10541240

OTHER BOOKS IN THE TO-GIVE-AND-TO-KEEP® SERIES:

Welcome to the New Baby
To a very special Daughter
To a very special Grandma
To a very special Mother-in-law
To a very special Grandpa
Happy Anniversary
To my very special Love
To a very special Mother
To a very special Son

To a very special Dad
To a very special Friend
To a very special Granddaughter
Wishing you Happiness
To my very special Husband
To someone very special
    Merry Christmas!
To a very special Sister
To my very special Wife

Dedicated to my own Aunty Mer, who has been like a second mother to me – Helen

Published simultaneously in 1998 by Exley Publications LLC in the USA and Exley Publications Ltd in Great Britain.

12 11 10 9 8 7 6 5 4 3 2 1

Written by Pam Brown
Pam Brown published with permission © Helen Exley 1998
Edited by Helen Exley
Illustrated by Juliette Clarke
Printed in China

Exley Publications Ltd, 16 Chalk Hill, Watford, Herts WD19 4BG, UK.
Exley Publications LLC, 185 Main Street, Spencer, MA 01562, USA.
www.helenexleygiftbooks.com

To a very special®
AUNT

WRITTEN BY PAM BROWN
ILLUSTRATED BY JULIETTE CLARKE

Everyone has places in their hearts
for special people – yours is so
snug – a place to keep the
best of memories.

A HELEN EXLEY GIFTBOOK

SO CLOSE, SO SPECIAL

Dear Aunt, dear special friend, dear holder of
secrets, dear giver of surprises –
I send you hugs and kisses to last you
through the year.
If you find you're running out, tell me.
I'll send you more by return of post.

...

Half of the happy memories of childhood
involve aunts.

...

There are very special aunts you only introduce to
very special friends.

...

Very small children don't just love the
shape and feel and sound of aunties,
but their individual smell.
Even the ones whose scent is garlic.

...

How lucky I am to have an aunt like you.
To think – some people haven't a single aunt to
their name. How do they manage?

...

I love you. My cat loves you.
My pet mouse loves you.
And I know you love us all back.

...

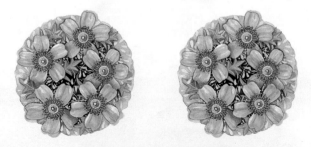

WHAT ARE AUNTS FOR?

Aunts are good for outings.

They aren't as strict as mothers – and they are more resilient than grandmas. They can be wheedled – just a bit. They are generally weak-willed when it comes to cream cakes and potato crisps.

They slow down to let you stroke cats on walls – and most of them talk Cat.

They always have wonderful excuses when you get home late.

…

What would you do without aunts.

They fill a gap that absolutely no one else fits.

…

An aunt is a bonus.

…

Aunts
are so useful for
sharing secrets.

...

Aunts are a sort of bridge between children and grown-ups. They don't belong to either side and so can arrange compromises.

...

It is a part of an aunt's duty, however old she may be, to become child-size for an afternoon.

...

When your aunt flops down, kicks off her shoes, shuts her eyes and only nods when you ask if she'd like a cup of tea – you know you've overdone it.

...

JUST PERFECT

There are women just born to be aunts, who know
by instinct when a cuddle is needed and when it
will encroach on dignity. When a kiss is necessary.
And a clean handkerchief. They have the capacity to
shrink to puppy-size, or mouse, or slithering snake
– when to expand to elephant or Fee Fi Fo Fum.
When to sing – and when to listen. When to dance
the polka. When to applaud. When to help with
homework. When to keep well back.
An aunt like this is good at being shut in the
cellar under the stairs – a dungeon, a cavern, a
place of ghosties – skilled in climbing rocks and
wading through icy streams.

A teller of tales. A willing goalkeeper.
Someone with a penchant for dressing up
and board games.
Someone guaranteed to be astounded and delighted
at the correct moments.
Someone who laughs and jokes and is
mystified by tricks.
Someone who completely understands about The
Little Girl Next Door.
Aunts such as these are rare – but hard-wearing.
Guaranteed to last a lifetime.
With a little bit of luck they'll be around to comfort
and enchant your children.

...

THEY SPOIL YOU ROTTEN

Aunts have Special Cookie Tins.

"You choose."

…

When parents hum and ha over a really
beautiful, really expensive, outfit for you –
it's often aunt who says "I'll go halves."

…

Aunts eat all your awful greens.

…

An aunt can persuade anyone that you're
old enough, clever enough, sensible enough
to go for the things you really want.

…

Aunts are inclined to side step your
mother's threatening glances – and buy you
another chocolate sundae with nuts,
whipped cream
and a cherry on the top.
After all – auntie goes home.
Mum mops up.

…

Aunts are the only people who can turn to
your mother or father and say
"Bosh! You did it when you were their age –
and it didn't do you any harm."

…

Aunts save you the biggest strawberry.

…

HAVING FUN

There are aunts who cheek
policemen.
And prod the produce on the
market stall.
Sing in public places.
Cool off in the
fountains.
And send back cups
with flaws.
Get into conversations
– everywhere
– with every one.
They drive you to despair
– but make you feel
fantastically alive.

…

How good to have an aunt – a grown-up who is
prepared to give up the status for an afternoon and
be the same age as yourself – only stronger,
and with a longer reach. Ideal for playing
Bears and Hide and Seek.
Able to gallop, crawl and wriggle.
A partner in the polka.
Someone who can squash into the Wendy House.
A giver of pick-a-backs.
A skimmer of stones. A horse to ride.
A pusher of swings. A rower of boats.
A teller of tales. A listener.
Aunts are invaluable.

...

She arrives on visits in a swirl of coat – small,
round, rosy, ageless – with her battered suitcase.
Has nothing. Has everything.
Is adored by the children.

...

WHAT MAKES A GOOD AUNT?

You can always tell a good aunt by the size
of her handbag.

It has to hold string and elastoplast, paper
and pencils and pens, small change for
mechanical rides outside shops, a little book
of wisdom, peppermints, paper handkerchiefs,
a whistle, scissors, face wipes,
a comb, hairgrips, scent, elastic bands,
a penknife, a thing for getting the tops off
bottles and a bag of bread for the ducks.

. . .

A good aunt earns her reputation and her title.

She does not smother you with kisses.

She does not gasp at the sight of you and say

"My! How you've grown!"

She remembers how old you are and does not give

you a pull-along dog when you are eight.

She is courteous to your toad

and interested in your collection of stones.

She is prepared to play beach cricket

– even if she can be a bit of an embarrassment.

She doesn't tell dad you had a Funny Half Hour in

Woolworths.

She does not mention afterwards

how tight you held her hand on the Ghost Train.

...

A good aunt is one who is always prepared to play

just one more game.

Even when her eyes are rolling slightly.

...

HONORARY AUNTS

There are people called aunt because
they are related.
There are people called aunt because dad says we've
got to call them so.
And there are people called aunt because they are
extra special and we love them very, very much.
(Sometimes all these are the same person).

...

They only really
qualify as aunts if
they are kind and
cuddly.

...

What would the world do without aunties? –
Aunties by relationship and aunties by love. An
extra card on birthdays. An extra hug when things
go well. A source of small surprises – and great
astonishments at times.

Bridges between close family and the
frightening wider world.

. . .

Aunts by adoption
– Prone to sit and chat to your mother in the
kitchen, or help her hang out the washing.
– Women your mother telephones when things go
wrong. Or extra right.
– Women who share your expeditions to the zoo
and beach and shopping.
– Women who take over in emergencies.
– Women we can trust.
Aunts, how bare our lives would be without them.

. . .

VERY SPECIAL PEOPLE

Long distance aunts can send love in envelopes
and kisses down the phone.

...

An aunt is a good investment if you go for a car
ride, train ride or a bus ride. They know lots and
lots of songs and rhymes and riddles.

...

The odd thing about aunts is that they never get
any older. Not inside at any rate.

...

By tradition, aunties are special people.

When we are very small they are the ladies with sweeties in their pockets, mint-new coins in their purses, knobbly packages in their carrier bags. Aunties understand the etiquette of dolls tea parties and always ask for another cup. Aunties actually eat wet pastry. Aunties allow themselves to be ridden as a pony. Aunties put money in your birthday card.

And as you grow older, aunties are the people who meet buses and trains and aircrafts, who take you out to tea in proper restaurants – and yet will share a bag of sticky buns on a park bench and feed the ducks.

Aunties come in all shapes, all sizes, all ages. Some know just about everything – and some know just about nothing, but make you laugh a lot.

Hurrah for aunties.

The world couldn't do without them.

…

THEY ADD SOMETHING EXTRA

Aunts pad out a family so nicely.

…

There's something so comfortable about the
word aunt.
It reassures us – we feel the arms of
family fold about us.

…

When your parents or brothers or sisters are
driving you dotty – an aunt can
give you respite.

…

A family without an aunt is a deprived family.

…

Aunts break through the carapace of a family unit –
and bring a breeze from the world outside.

…

CRAZY! ZANY!

Ladies who look quite dull have a mad streak they
only reveal to nephews and nieces.

…

Rain cannot stop an aunt. Or flood or fire. Nothing
can withstand a determined and enthusiastic
member of the species.
And we will remember. Pizzas and cakes in a
steamed-up jalopy. A boat entangled in a willow.
The giant roller-coaster.
Aunts are a very good thing.

…

It is not the Aunts who Bear Gifts
that are always the most popular.
It is more likely to be the Aunt who can
turn cartwheels. Or waggle her ears.

…

Why is it that aunts are so often larger than life?
A race of mild eccentrics.

Everyone needs a frivolous auntie.

An auntie who drinks coffee at the Ritz.

An auntie who walks all day

and never falters. And wears a hat with feathers.

An auntie who can stop taxis, dead.

An auntie who always has bread crusts

for the ducks.

An auntie that winks at policemen

Everyone should go on a jaunt with one.

...

PROTECTOR, COMFORTER

There's a comfortable feeling in the house
when your aunt is there. As though she's
scooped you up and taken you back in
time, to when you were small.

…

An aunt is a very welcoming
port in any storm.

…

Aunts are the people who comfort you
when you are in the dog-house and
whisper that your parents did
just the same.

…

It's good to have an aunt.

She is like a dear familiar island,

promising shelter

in times of stress or sorrow.

...

When things have been going wrong there

is nothing like a good aunt for taking off

the pressure.

...

A good aunt can always organise a

memorable funeral for your dear,

dead mouse.

...

<u>LIFELONG FRIENDS</u>

Good aunts are not affected by time.

They go on being kind and cuddly all your life

– or as much of it as they can manage.

...

Aunts can be a source of constant joy.

You can lock them in wardrobes. And try on their
shoes. And search for the little bags of sweets that
they've hidden round the house. Or make them
play soldiers. And tell them your riddles.

And sing them your songs.

And then you can sleep all the way home in the car.
Auntie, of course, would love to go to bed – but
there are all those marbles, and sticky tumblers and
half eaten biscuits and toys on the stairs....

She smiles sleepily,

but promises herself – no glitter paint next time.

. . .

Here you are, the very best of aunts and
falling into no category – being utterly yourself.

Unpredictable, amusing, kind.

A source of surprises. The best of companions.

Ageless. Friend.

. . .